SWEDEN

LETTERS FROM AROUND THE WORLD

Polly Goodman

Photographs by Howard Davies

CHERRYTREE BOOKS

LETTERS FROM AROUND THE WORLD

Titles in this series

AUSTRALIA · BANGLADESH · BRAZIL · CANADA · CHINA
COSTA RICA · EGYPT · FRANCE · GERMANY · GREECE
INDIA · INDONESIA · ITALY · JAMAICA · JAPAN · KENYA
MEXICO · NIGERIA · PAKISTAN · RUSSIA · SAUDI ARABIA
SOUTH AFRICA · SPAIN · SWEDEN · THE USA

A Cherrytree Book

Conceived and produced by

Nutshell
MEDIA

www.nutshellmedialtd.co.uk

VISIT OUR WEBSITE www.evansbooks.co.uk

First published in 2007 by
Evans Brothers Ltd
2A Portman Mansions
Chiltern Street
London W1U 6NR

Consultant: Lena Johansson
Designer: Tim Mayer
Map artwork: Encompass Graphics Ltd
All other artwork: Tim Mayer

All photographs were taken by Howard Davies, apart from page 27, which is courtesy of Anna Yu/AY Images.

Acknowledgements
The photographer would like to thank Mathias Nyström and his family, Matilda Graflund, Maria Abrahamsson, the staff and pupils of Rönnbyskolan School, Västerås, Marie-Louise Ohlander, Tom and Lotta Svensson at the Båtsuoj Sami Centre, Greta Huuva, Lena Lindholm Sköld and Kajsa Bengtz at the Västerås Domkyrkan and the Västerås First Plaza for all their help.

British Library Cataloguing in Publication Data
Goodman, Polly
  Letters from Sweden. – (Letters from around the world)
  1. Sweden – Social life and customs – Juvenile literature
  I. Title
948.5'06

ISBN-13: 9781842344361

Cover: Mathias (back, right) with his two brothers Erik (back, left) and Edvin (front), and their friend Matilda, on a bridge over the Svartån river, in Västerås.
Title page: On the trampoline in front of Mathias's house.
This page: This lake in northern Sweden freezes over from October until May each year.
Contents page: Mathias with Edvin and his best friend Matilda.
Glossary page: The sign marking the location of the Arctic Circle in northern Sweden.
Further Information page: A reindeer with her ten-day-old calf, which belong to a Sami reindeer herder.
Index: Rapids on the Storforsen river in northern Sweden.

Contents

My Country

Wednesday, 2 March

23 Pine Tree Street
72464 Västerås
Sweden

Dear Toni,

Hej! (You say 'Hey'. This means 'hello' in Swedish, my language.)

My name is Mathias Nyström (say 'Mat-ee-us Nee-strum'), but you can call me Mat. I'm 9 years old and I live in a city called Västerås (say 'Vester-orse'), in Sweden. I've got two brothers, Erik who's 12 and Edvin, who's 5 years old. My mum's name is Kristina and my dad's is Per.

It's great to have a penpal to help me practise my English.

Write back soon!

From

Mathias

Here's my family, outside our house. The sign on the door means 'Welcome to Kristina and Per's house'.

Sweden is the largest country in Scandinavia. People have lived there since ancient times. Over 1,000 years ago, it was home to people called the Vikings, who explored and raided parts of Europe.

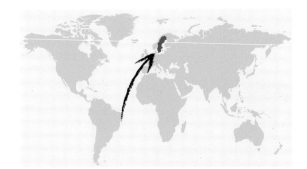

Sweden's place in the world.

0   100   200   300 kilometres

0   50   100   150 miles

Kebnekaise
2,111m

KÖLEN MOUNTAINS

Arctic Circle

Norwegian Sea

N

FINLAND

SWEDEN

Lake Storsjön

Gulf of Bothnia

Lake Siljan

NORWAY

Klar-Gota

Sweden is in northern Europe, between Norway and Finland. The Arctic Circle runs across the north of the country.

Uppsala

Västerås

Lake Mälaren

Örebro

STOCKHOLM

Lake Hjälmaren

Lake Vänern

ESTONIA

Skagerrak

Lake Vättern

Norrköping

Linköping

Göteborg

Jönköping

North Sea

Gotland

Kattegat

Öland

LATVIA

Helsingborg

DENMARK

Malmö

Baltic Sea

LITHUANIA

Västerås is one of the oldest cities in Sweden. Here you can see the cathedral and the Old Town (the oldest part of the city) in the background.

Västerås is a big city in south-east Sweden. It is about 100 kilometres from Stockholm, the capital. People have lived in Västerås since before the Vikings. The Vikings built burial mounds at a place called Anundshög, just outside the city.

Västerås is beside a huge lake, called Lake Mälaren. It is the third-largest lake in Sweden and it stretches all the way to Stockholm. The River Svartån runs through the city centre into the lake.

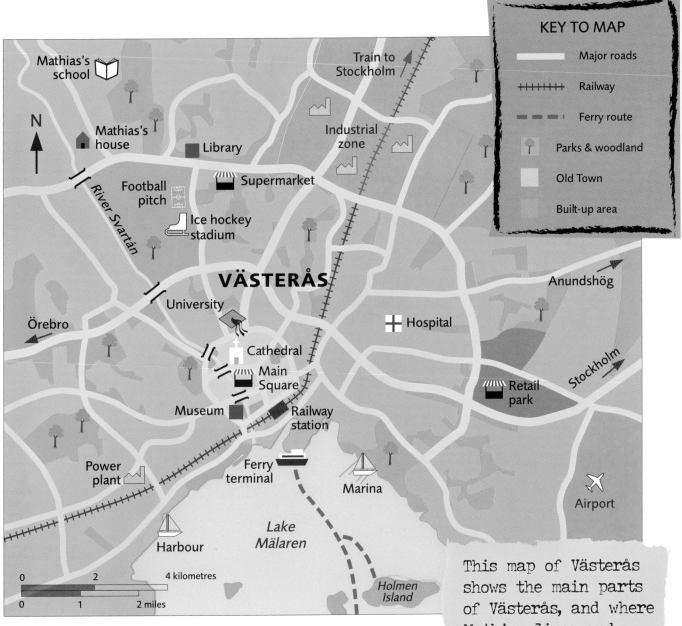

KEY TO MAP

————	Major roads
+++++++	Railway
- - - - -	Ferry route
⊤	Parks & woodland
▢	Old Town
▢	Built-up area

Mathias's school

N

Mathias's house

Library

Train to Stockholm

Industrial zone

Football pitch

Supermarket

Ice hockey stadium

VÄSTERÅS

University

Örebro

Anundshög

Hospital

Cathedral

Main Square

Stockholm

Retail park

Museum

Railway station

Power plant

Ferry terminal

Marina

Airport

Harbour

Lake Mälaren

Holmen Island

0	2	4 kilometres
0	1	2 miles

This map of Västerås shows the main parts of Västerås, and where Mathias lives and goes to school.

About 800 years ago, a big cathedral was built in Västerås. It still stands in the old part of the city. There is also a monastery, a university and a large shopping centre. Machinery and other goods are made in industrial areas of the city. Large ships are loaded and unloaded in the harbour on the lakeside. It is the largest freshwater harbour in Scandinavia.

Landscape and Weather

The area around Västerås, like most of Sweden, is flat or made up of rolling hills. There are mountains in the north-west, on the border with Norway. Much of Sweden is covered in forests and there are many lakes.

In the forests of northern Sweden, drivers have to watch out for reindeer on the roads.

The south of Sweden has a temperate climate, with short, cold days in the winter and longer, warmer days in the summer. Further north it is much colder. North of the Arctic Circle, the sun never rises for part of the winter and never sets for part of the summer.

North of the Arctic
Circle, it is so cold that
lakes like this one stay
frozen from October to
May each year.

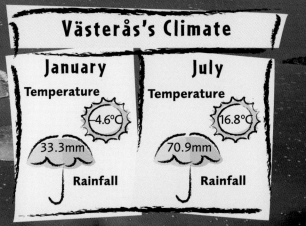

Västerås's Climate

January	July
Temperature	**Temperature**
-4.6°C	16.8°C
33.3mm	70.9mm
Rainfall	**Rainfall**

At Home

Mathias's house is in a suburb of Västerås, about 15 minutes from the city centre by bike. The suburb was only built about 40 years ago on farmland and woodland. As Västerås grew bigger, new suburbs like this one were built around the city.

Like many houses in Sweden, Mathias's house is built from wood. It has its own postbox, on the street outside, and a trampoline in the front garden.

The house is on the edge of some woods. Sometimes Mathias sees foxes, hares and even deer in the back garden. The deer come to eat the flowers.

Mathias and his brothers play a game of cards in the living room. One of their favourite games is Scrabble™, which is called *Alfapet* (alphabet) in Swedish.

Inside, there is a living room and a big kitchen on the ground floor. Upstairs, there are five bedrooms and a bathroom. Mathias, Edvin and Erik each have their own bedroom, and there is a separate room for guests.

The brothers each have their own desk and computer in their bedroom. Mathias has posters of his favourite ice-hockey teams on his walls.

Edvin helps his dad prepare the vegetable patch, where they will grow potatoes, carrots and lettuce.

Outside, there is a garage and a shed, where bicycles, skis and garden tools are stored. The family also put used paper, glass and tins there before taking them to the recycling station. At the side of the house, there is a wooden deck for barbecues in the summer.

In the back garden, Mathias and Erik practise some football skills.

Tuesday, 10 April

23 Pine Tree Street
72464 Västerås
Sweden

Hej Toni!

Have I told you about our new trampoline? My brothers and I bought it a few weeks ago. We had to wash Mum and Dad's cars every week for a year to save up enough money. Lots of our friends have one, too. We go on it after school and see who can bounce the highest. I can almost do a somersault, like Erik. We need to put it away before the winter because it would get covered in snow, but I play ice hockey after school then so I won't miss it that much.

What do you do at home after school?

Hej då! (Bye!)

Mathias

Here's Erik and me on the trampoline. Erik can usually get higher than me but I'm going to catch up soon!

Food and Mealtimes

For breakfast, Mathias and his brothers usually have muesli or porridge, followed by rye bread or crispbreads with cheese, tomato, cold meats and pickled cucumber. Sometimes they have fruit and yoghurt. The boys drink fruit juice or milk at breakfast. Their mum and dad drink black coffee.

Mathias and Erik eat their breakfast in the kitchen. There are crispbreads in the basket.

At school, Mathias and his classmates collect their lunch from the canteen and eat it in their classroom.

For dinner, the family eats fish, sausages or other meat, with potatoes and vegetables or salad. In the winter they usually have hot potatoes. In the summer they have salad. For dessert, they have strawberries and ice cream or blueberry pie.

In the summer, when it is warm enough, Mathias and his family cook outside on the barbecue.

At the weekly open market, Mathias, Erik and their father buy some pineapples and plums. The prices are shown in Swedish krona.

Mathias's family buy most of their food at a big supermarket, about a kilometre away from their house. But if they are in town at the weekend, they pick up some fruit at the open market in the main square.

A favourite lunch at the weekend is meatballs with potatoes and salad. Crispbreads and cheese are usually on the table with every meal.

Saturday, 20 April

23 Pine Tree Street
72464 Västerås
Sweden

Hej Toni!

You asked me for a typical Swedish recipe. Here's how to make one of my favourite dishes: meatballs.

You will need: 400g minced pork, 3 tablespoons grated onion, 4 tablespoons breadcrumbs, 100ml water or milk, 2 teaspoons cornflour, 1 egg, salt and pepper to taste.

1. In a bowl, gradually add the water or milk to the cornflour, stirring well.
2. Mix in the rest of the ingredients, apart from the meat, and leave for 5 minutes. Then mix in the meat.
3. Roll the mixture into small balls and fry them in a frying pan for 15 minutes, turning every few minutes so they are brown all over.
4. Serve with potatoes, gravy and some lingonberry jam (if you can't find any lingonberry jam, use cranberry jelly instead).

From

Mathias

Here's a plate of meatballs I made with Mum, cooked to perfection!

School Day

Mathias cycles to school and back with Erik. They leave the house just before 8 a.m. and get to school, ready to start lessons, at 8.10 a.m. They ride on a cycle lane all the way to school.

Lessons run from 8.10 a.m. until 11.10 a.m, when there is a break for lunch. They start again at midday and finish at 2.10 p.m. Most children stay on for an after-school club, which is open until 5.30 p.m.

Mathias and Erik cycle to school most days. If there is heavy snow or it is very cold, their mum drives them in the car.

In an English lesson,
Mathias's class plays a game
about the parts of the body.

Mathias has lessons in maths,
geography, natural sciences,
IT, art and Swedish. He has
just started to learn English.
Next year, when he is 10, he
can choose to learn a third
language: either Spanish,
Italian or German.

Mathias practises his computer
skills in the computer room.
All the pupils have IT lessons
three or four times a week.

Mathias started school when he was 6 years old. Like most Swedish children, when he is 15, he will go to a college called a *gymnasium* for three years. Then, when he is 18 or 19, he hopes to go to university.

Wednesday, 5 May

23 Pine Tree Street
72464 Västerås
Sweden

Hej!

I'm glad you liked the meatballs. Can you send me one of your favourite recipes soon?

Today at school we worked on the school garden. We grow vegetables and flowers there every year. It's too cold to grow much in the winter. At the beginning of spring, we pull out all the weeds and give the soil a good rake, ready for planting. Next week, we're going to plant the seeds. We're going to grow potatoes and onions, as well as some sunflowers.

Do you grow anything at school?

Write soon!

Mathias

Here I am with my classmates, digging out the weeds in our school garden.

Off to Work

Like most families in Sweden, both of Mathias's parents work. His dad works for a finance company in Örebro, a town 60 kilometres from Västerås. It takes him an hour to drive there every day. Mathias's mum is a social worker in Västerås. She cycles to work every day, like many people in the city.

Mathias's mum talks to another social worker about the week ahead.

This timber has just been cut. It is ready to be collected and taken to a factory to be made into pulp.

Many people in Sweden work in industries to do with timber. Some make paper, while others make things from wood. There are also large Swedish companies making machinery, motor vehicles, and iron and steel products.

Many people take the train to work in Sweden. This train is taking commuters from Stockholm to the cities of Norrköping and Malmö.

Free Time

Mathias plays lots of different sports and games, although his favourite by far is ice hockey. In the spring, summer and autumn, he and his brothers play football and ride their bikes. In the winter, when he isn't playing ice hockey, Mathias and his friends like making snowcastles and going tobogganing.

In the summer, Mathias and his brothers have football practice every weekend. Edvin is practising some football skills.

Mathias is learning to drive the family's boat. They use it to go fishing and to visit islands in the lake.

Saturday, 15 November

23 Pine Tree Street
72464 Västerås
Sweden

Hej!

Today I played in an ice-hockey match and we won! The score was 5:3 so it was pretty close. I play in a team at the local ice-hockey stadium. We practise four times a week throughout the winter. Each session lasts an hour, but it takes at least 15 minutes just to put on and take off all the padded clothing, so it usually takes about 2 hours in all. I like being part of a team and having to concentrate for every second of practice time. If I don't, I know I might let the rest of the team down.

Do you play any team games? Write back and tell me about them.

Hej då!

Mathias →

Here I am in my ice-hockey gear. I wear a full-face helmet, with pads on my legs, knees, elbows, shoulders and neck. I wear padded trousers and gloves, too!

Religion and Festivals

Most people in Sweden are Christians and belong to the Lutheran Church. There are also some Catholics, Baptists and Orthodox Christians, as well as Muslims, Jews and Buddhists. Not many people in Sweden go to church regularly, but they celebrate important ceremonies, such as christenings and confirmations. There are also many pagan traditions in Sweden.

These two girls have just been confirmed in a Lutheran church. They are reading a passage from the Bible with the help of a female priest.

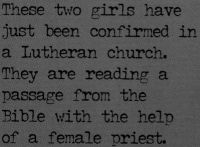

Every Easter, Mathias and his brothers draw patterns on eggs with coloured felt pens. They eat the eggs for breakfast and dinner on Easter Sunday.

The main festivals in Sweden are Christmas, Easter, Lucia and Midsummer. At Lucia, on 13 December, children take part in a church ceremony. All dressed in white, they walk in a procession carrying candles. In the morning, they get up early and take coffee and saffron buns to their parents.

At the Midsummer festival in June, people dress in traditional costume. They sing and dance around a maypole decorated with leaves and flowers.

27

Fact File

Flag: Blue, with a yellow cross nearest the side of the flagpole.

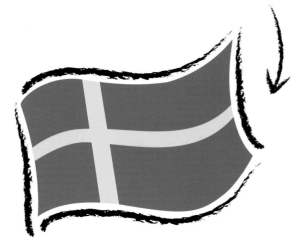

Capital city: Stockholm. The oldest part of the city, the Old Town (above), was built in medieval times.

Other major cities: Göteborg, Malmö, Uppsala, Västerås.

Size: 449,964km².

Population: 9,016,596.

Languages: The main language in Sweden is Swedish. The Sami and Finnish people also speak their own languages.

Longest river: Klar-Göta (719km).

Highest mountain: Mount Kebnekaise (2,111m).

Main industries: Iron and steel, hi-tech machinery, wood and paper products, processed food, motor vehicles.

Currency: Swedish krona (SKr), divided into öre (1 krona=100 öre).

Sami: The Sami people have lived in northern Sweden, Norway and Finland for thousands of years. Some Sami people still make a living from traditional occupations such as herding reindeer.

Vikings: From the 9th to the 11th centuries, the Vikings lived in Sweden, Norway and Denmark. They buried dead warriors, kings and priests in mounds decorated with big stones (below).

European Union: In 2005, Sweden joined the European Union (EU).

Main religions: About 87 per cent of the population are Lutheran. The rest are Roman Catholic, Orthodox, Baptist, Muslim, Jewish or Buddhist.

Main festivals: Christmas, Easter, Lucia (13 December), Midsummer.

Famous Swedes: ABBA was a Swedish pop music group from 1972 to 1982 that has sold about 300 million records. Björn Borg (born 1956) was a champion tennis player who won Wimbledon five times in a row from 1976 to 1980. Sven-Göran Eriksson was manager of England's national football team from 2001 to 2006.

Stamps: Swedish stamps show famous people or current affairs, such as membership of the EU.

Glossary

Arctic Circle An imaginary line that runs around the northern regions of the world.

confirmation A special ceremony to celebrate a person joining the Church.

crispbreads Flat, dry biscuits made from rye flour.

European Union (EU) A group of countries in Europe that work and trade together.

harbour A place where ships can load and unload.

Hej! This means 'Hi!' in Swedish.

Hej då! This means 'Bye!' in Swedish.

lingonberry A type of cranberry (a red berry) that grows wild in the forests of northern Scandinavia and is used to make lingonberry jam.

Midsummer A celebration of the summer solstice in June.

pagan A person who has different religious beliefs to the world's main religions.

population All the people who live in one place, like a country or a city.

pulp A material made from wood. It is used to make paper.

Scandinavia A region made up of Denmark, Sweden and Norway.

social worker A person who helps people with disadvantages, such as disability or poverty.

stadium A sports ground surrounded with seats for spectators.

suburb A district at the edge of a town or city.

Vikings Seafaring warriors from northern Europe, who raided parts of Europe between the 9th and the 11th centuries.

temperate Neither extremely hot nor extremely cold.

traditional Something that has been done for a long time.

Further Information

Information books:

The Changing Face of Sweden by Stephen Keeler (Wayland, 2004)

Continents: Europe by Leila Foster and Mary Fox (Heinemann, 2006)

Eyewitness Travel Guides: Sweden by Ulf Johansson and Forlag Streiffert (Dorling Kindersley, 2005)

Geography Fact Files: Polar Regions by Paul Mason (Hodder Wayland, 2004)

Habitats: Around the Poles by Robert Snedden (Franklin Watts, 2004)

Swedish Food and Cooking by Anna Mosesson (Aquamarine, 2006)

Fiction:

The Best of Pippi Longstocking by Astrid Lingren (OUP, 2003). Follows the amazing adventures of a funny and incredibly strong girl.

The Queen's Necklace: A Swedish Folktale by Jane Langton (Hyperion, 1994)

Swedish Folk Tales by John Bauer (Floris Books, 2004)

Tales from Moominvalley by Tove Jannson (Farrar Straus Giroux, 1995). Follows the adventures of small, fat, shy creatures called Moomins.

Websites:

Visit Sweden
www.visitsweden.com/
The official travel guide with photos, information and pronunciation guides.

The World Factbook
www.cia.gov/cia/publications/factbook/
Facts and figures about Sweden and other countries.

Index